CW01046163

Thinking in Ink

A collection of colourscapes

A. L. Magnone

First published 2016
Ratbot Publishing
Manchester, UK
www.ratbotpublishing.com

ISBN: 978-0-9955137-1-6

Printed in the U.K.

Ratbot publishing is a trading name of Waveform
Computing Ltd

For Dan, without whom this could never have been.

Introduction

Synaesthesia is defined as a condition where experiencing a sensation in one sense triggers a sensation in another – for me, I experience emotions as colours.

I wrote my first colourscape three years ago as an assignment for my second year Creative Writing class – I called it *Diurnal*, and I used a blend of all colours to create a narrative that described (what at the time was) the cyclical nature of my depression. It was the first time I had admitted to myself that something wasn't right, and writing was the best way I could express this.

Since then, I have begun an MA in Creative Writing, been prescribed medication, read numerous books on mental health and conversed with two different therapists.

I often over-think, but I can slow down if I'm putting words to paper – I started my individual colourscapes simply as a way of not letting my emotions overwhelm me. It was really the idea of a fellow MA student, Louise, that I should collate these pieces into a book.

It's nerve-wracking to create something based on purely my own personality and experiences, but why shouldn't we be honest about our emotions? My style is quite abstract, and it reflects my thoughts and emotions as truly and honestly as possible. Each colourscape is accompanied by an essay to help decode the abstraction, and to provide a clearer insight into each emotion.

I've listed my colourscapes in chronological order of them being written. I never thought that these would become anything other than notes on my fluctuating personality. Everything here has been written since I began taking medication, as initially that gave me a huge creative block and I had to force myself back into the habit of writing so I didn't lose that side of myself.

My essays are frank and honest, even at the toughest moments. I decided to bare all because I know how painful it can be to feel alone. Alone and ashamed. If anyone reading this feels or has ever felt the same way, I want you to know that you don't need to feel ashamed anymore – your thoughts and actions aren't selfish, they're desperate. At your lowest moments, you might not see the other side, and after you might regret your past feelings; don't. Mental health problems have plagued humanity forever, and you do not need to feel ashamed. Remember, you are loved.

This book has been terrifying and exhilarating to produce, and I've poured my whole self into it. If it helps even one person – gives them hope, strength, or insight into their own struggles, for we all have them – it will have been worth it.

I am grey.

Some think that grey is unease,
conflict,   difficulty.
Perhaps it is.
                    It is also n o t h i n g.

White is too pure, unaltered to cradle
the dead-weight burden of   nothing.

Light grey, wisps like mists of the moor. I
am here, but only just.
                    I am real, but only just.

Mist weighs heavier on your skin than raindrops.

                                    I am a parody
My heart trembles while my   of
pulse cannot match up.   The Thinker,
                                    frozen into grey.
    Solid now,
anchored to the ground by the n o t h i n g
that has permeated my flesh.
                                                        S
                                                        o
                                                        l
                                                        i
The world around is green and brown,   d
flashes of golden yellow shot through   i
with piercing cries of young at play.   f
                                                        y
I am rooted; yet, like any deadened bough, with life   i
comes buds.   n
    Piercing harder than any cry, I am shot through   g
    with silver and my heart   b r e a t h e s.

                        I am heavy,
                            I am chains,
I am the silver birch and the moon.   I am cold.

No colour is ever what it seems in the
        ever-changing light,
                        and,
                        in the dusk
                                    I shine.

GREY – or Emptiness, heaviness, weightlessness, and feeling like you're somehow not really real

I wrote this piece the very first time I went camping – it was a group activity, and it was such a fun weekend, despite me having to go to work on the Saturday. But late on Sunday, I just started fading away. I didn't know what was happening, and I just wanted to run away. I went and sat by the edge of the fishing pond for a long time. I felt frozen.

Dan (my husband, then fiancé) tried to talk to me, but I didn't feel as if I could. So I asked for paper and a pen and I wrote this. The original is on the back of a folded printout of a route map – the second page and last four directions of the campsite to Greenfield in Oldham, with the nearest train station. The blue biro had bent in the warmth of the sun on our car's dashboard.

Feeling grey is like sensing a storm in the air. The weather is beautiful, clear and calm, but there is such a sensation of built-up energy electrifying the air. Like feeling tears behind your eyes and in your throat, not really attempting to hold them back, but not knowing when they will burst.

In the end, reality brought me back to myself. Instead of the storm breaking, the clouds simply rolled away. Grey didn't always end so calmly in those days, but it did then. I think it might even be because I chose to write; I took a step back and looked at the situation. I counted to ten and breathed. I didn't feel like I was trying to break free of the chains.

But I did.

I look to my own ring of gold. I am safe. I can see the storm clouds ahead, but the yellow softens them, makes them safe. Hushes them to wait, slow. Not today they say. I envelop my mind in the brushed cotton clouds as we rattle along. Here I can rest, beside myself. Here I can rest, beside me. At peace. Voices echo through the silence and I feel a gentle hum beside me. Musky darkness still teases the horizon, but threaded through with ribbons of gold. The sunlight powders the tips of the clouds with warmth. I am that pale yellow. Soft and warm. I love when you cannot see the sun. My eyes, desperate for colour, will prickle with static until I look away. I don't believe in the beauty of a cloudless sky.

YELLOW-GREY – or Nostalgia, or safety and the hope of something better

The weekend away to Whitby was very spur of the moment, trying to take my mind off the events of that week. It was the first week I had done serious damage to myself.

I had self-harmed before I started the medication as a way to take control of my thoughts, carefully concentrating on healing in order to maintain that level of control. Only ever superficial, by absolute choice. It was something I was attempting to stop, with reasonable success. But in the first few months of 2015, I was all over the place. A silly argument and too much wine sent my thoughts spiralling out of control, and drunk people don't always make the best decisions.

Afterwards, bandaged up and scared of myself, I needed a distraction, desperately. So we went to Whitby.

As we drove in our beaten-up old Micra that we called The General, the sky was beautiful: brilliant golden sun shining in streaks through grey tufted clouds. I found some paper – page 1 of 2 of those same campsite directions. Despite the intensity of the preceding days, I felt calm and safe in our rattling car and in the remembrance of happiness.

Not long engaged, and with my staunchest supported by my side, I felt safe.

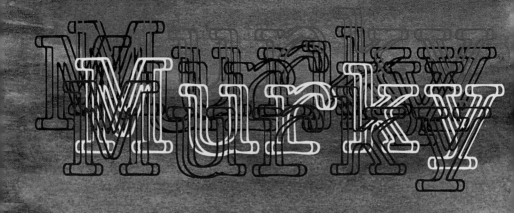

Murky

I can't see what the colours may be through the
smog. The mundane viscosity, one plodding foot after
another, heavily bursting each vacuumed step before
sealing down once more with a shuck. It is a swamp, I
can feel it. Half expected gas lamps shine in my
distance, teasing me. Even if I did not know better
than to follow them, I couldn't. I am a willow, rooted
and weeping. The air is close; it breathes with me.

What dusk is dusk? I lose my senses in the dirge of
murky colours. No time, no time. However, I never
feel alone. I am surrounded, other rooted trees and
swamp-stricken survivors. We are each to our own
but it is ... comforting? The close air breathes
me, rising and falling my chest. I close my eyes.

MURKY – or Feeling stuck and breathless, and feeling hopeless about the present

Office environments aren't what I like best – stuck at a computer all day is quite draining on my emotions. I've only ever held one office job, an HR position, glued to a headset phone and screen all day long.

I was so grateful for an opportunity to have a job after I graduated university, but it was difficult, precisely because it wasn't. Reading a script and typing answers verbatim, fifteen minutes at a time (I was always slightly over target, I'm too chatty), four times an hour, thirty times a day. Day after day after day.

Some days were slow; one of those days I felt as if I would drown in the stale air if I didn't write. I either couldn't breathe or felt like there was too much air for me to handle. The original is jotted on a torn-off sheet from my work notebook, one side listing a few strings of numbers, and notes of any comfort breaks (12:33 – 12:37; 4mins).

I am very grateful to the office workers that make up the backbone of our country: keeping companies running, filing tax returns, writing insurance policies, answering 999 calls. (I'm not talking about cold-calling.) That is something I could never do. Two months in an office nearly wore a hole in my nerves, so to those that don't give up – thank you.

Glittering Shimmering Starbursts

and opalescent scattered showers

raindrops of colour
mottle and evaporate
together

ALWAYS PERFECT YET NEVER ENOUGH
AND SOMEHOW TOO MUCH

(somehow)

After,
an oyster lies open, its
thick pink tongue bedding
a tiny   pearl.
Iridescent
with echoes of its
birth.

Creation
is
wonderful,

but,   bridges itself with downy fear.
like all   The fear of the broken oyster.
wonder,   The clouded pearl.
                              Not yet ripe.

A sigh.

Warm and awakened.

Waiting.

GLITTER – or Pink skies at night are always delightful

My titles are rather wordy because I find it hard to pack down each thought, emotion, or feeling into just one or two words. I presented a few colourscapes to my MA workshop class to test the waters – I had no idea how they would be received.

My tutor, Nick, asked if there were none at all that could be encapsulated in a single word. It was difficult – but perhaps this one could. This one, written half-dazed in pencil on a page of an old exercise book. That word? Orgasm.

I would be lying if I didn't say that this colourscape didn't turn my cheeks the colour of its text, but I feel that it's just as important as any other to include this. Sex is such a part of society, yet, since the late Georgian era, we've collectively been sweeping the idea under the carpet. But if our neighbours, colleagues, friends and family are pregnant – often a great conversation-starter and source of all-round cheer – well, how else did they get that way?

We're a way off starting a family yet – I'd rather finish my Master's first! – but I do feel broody. I love visiting friends with babies, and seeing them always makes my heart ache with longing. But, what with my medication, I'm so scared of something going wrong. I'm sure this is a fear that resonates with any expecting parent, but that's the reasoning behind any lingering melancholy in this piece. The rest? That's for me to know!

STEADINESS IS HARD TO EXPLAIN. IT'S NOT EXACTLY A COLOUR. IT
BELONGS TO NATURE AND IS VISIBLE EVEN ON THE COLDEST,
GLOOMIEST MORNING. THE DOMINANT COLOUR IS BROWN,
BUT THE MAGICAL THING ABOUT STEADINESS IS THAT IT
IS REFLECTIVE. IT HELPS YOU SEE YOURSELF,
UNDERSTAND THAT YOU ARE STRONGER THAN YOU
LET YOURSELF BELIEVE AND THAT YOU CAN
WEATHER THE STORM. I AM THE TEAL DUCK
BOBBING ON A GLASSY MOAT. I AM THE
PAIR OF CANADA GEESE PATROLLING THE
WATER. I AM EACH AND EVERY TREE -
OAK, PINE, CHESTNUT, SYCAMORE -
DECIDEDLY DECIDUOUS, SHAKING MY
RUSSET CURLS AND WATCHING THE
LEAVES FALL. CAUGHT IN A BLIZZARD
OF LEAVES, THE WIND WHIPS AND
WHIRLS THEM FROM THE GROUND,
FORBIDDEN TO SETTLE. ALMOST MORE
ALIVE, FLOATING ALOFT THE BREEZE, NO
LONGER CHAINED BY STEM AND TWIG, I
WONDER WHAT COLOUR I SHALL BE WHEN I
TWIST MYSELF FREE OF MY HANGING STEM.
THE LEAVES HAVE SO MANY FACES THAT DANCE
BEFORE MY EYES - WATERY-EYED GRANDMOTHERS,
DISCONTENTED ADOLESCENTS, ABSENT-MINDED
STEPFATHERS, CANCER-RIDDEN COUSINS. NOT EVERYONE
GROWS OLD. SOME LEAVES FALL STILL GREEN, WHEREAS A
WITHERED MAHOGANY-COLOURED MAPLE MAY STILL CLING TO
ITS BOUGH. ONCE UPON A TIME I WOULD HAVE WEPT FOR THOSE
LEAVES BUT NOW, I DON'T KNOW. I CAN'T UNSEE THEIR BEAUTY. I
SAW A FAMILY BEFORE, THROWING PILES OF LEAVES AT ONE ANOTHER
IN LIEU OF SNOWBALLS. ALL METAPHORS ARE IMPERFECT. BUT THAT
MOMENT WAS. I AM THE BREADCRUMBS THROWN BY A SMILING CHILD TO
A PADDLE OF EAGER DUCKS. I AM THE LEAVES THRUST INTO A NOT-
QUITE UNSUSPECTING FACE. I AM EACH AND EVERY TREE THAT BIRTHS
AND SHEDS, YEAR ON YEAR, EPHEMERAL.
I LIVE.

BROWN – or Steadiness; the safety of rumination without the fear of thoughts turning black

After my brief stint in an office, my next job was out in the open. I've always adored preservation, restoration, and everything else that the National Trust stands for, so to be able to work for that charity is such a pleasure. Even as a simple car park attendant at Dunham Massey, I was so much more relaxed in an environment that felt *real*.

Days could be hot and sunny, tremendously busy, counting in almost two thousand cars, vans, campers and motorbikes in a six hour day! But days could be brutally cold, where the chill would reach my chest through seven layers of clothing, and the snow blew into my hut. Mostly, though, the days were fine and calm, with a steady stream of staff and visitors. On one calm and quiet autumn afternoon, I wrote this from my daydreams.

This was written on three sheets of quartered A4 paper, in this case being a print-out of an email. We recycled all papers containing non-confidential information as notepaper, so a few sheets out of a perpetually refilling stack now contain my steady thoughts.

Azure

is a beautiful word

but the romantic in me

favours powder blue.

It feels delicate on the lips, not fruity and exotic.

I am not a beach sky in the Mediterranean.

I am an English meadow.

My thoughts are scrunched into tight

little origami dragonflies, ricocheting through me.

I am a young soul drifting through an old life.

After a summer storm the sky may clear

to the inspiration of Turner -

he could never stand me.

Men and their mothers.

I do not feel real.

I am so living and yet so still.

I feel like a shook bottle

laid out

in the sun.

Will I fizz or

am I flat?

I am

Schrödinger's

soda.

BLUE – or Happiness is an elusive and unusual sensation; how long will it last?

Gorgeous summer days are something we arguably don't get enough of in North-West England, but the day I wrote this it was. I'm not a big summer bunny; I don't like humidity, and constantly reapplying factor 50+ sunscreen is a pain. But I love how it seems to bring everyone together.

Families picnic in the park, outdoor seating at delis and cafés are overflowing, and there seems like nowhere better for the adults than a pretty beer garden with a patch of sunshine.

That's where I wrote this colourscape: I was waiting for Dan to come home after work, but he texted me to meet him at the pub because the weather was so glorious. I ordered a G&T and found myself the perfect table – enough sun for him, but coolly dappled shade for me. And while I waited, I wrote.

A feeling of hurried enjoyment permeated the crowd; quick, have fun before the storm comes! And that's exactly how it felt to me. I never knew when my next storm would come, so it was so important to embrace any brief rays of sunshine while they lasted. But there was always that fizz beneath the surface of my thoughts, hinting that not everything was what it seemed.

The shape
of my heart is the fifth of
November. I often write of the darkness,
but I realise that I have long been wrong. It is
not the darkness that is so bleak. It is the
indecipherability. Like a fine grey mist clouding my
way, darkness is only to fear when unconquerable. I
feel like I finally understand. The tempest of my soul has
finally begun to ease to let me see the shapes underneath,
and that shape is the fifth of November. Darkness and I are
intrinsically linked, for one and for all. But I am not cloudy
no. I burn. I am life and I choose to revel in it. I watch the
tips of lurid orange lick at the sky over hundreds of silhouetted
heads, all so tall, my head thrown so far back in the hope of a
glimpse of my heart. I am not the fire. Sometimes I contain
fire, but I am not strong enough to fuel the flames eternal. I
am the embers thrown out by the flames that catch in the
breeze and whisk upwards, alighting into the sky. The
precious jewels encased by dusk, carelessly dancing
without thought, nor mind, nor want. I am the
navy-black sky often pensive
knowingly anxious. I am laced
with flecks of wondrous beauty,
things I once thought were my
only hope against the
darkness. But I know

I know that I cannot be only the
fiery echoes, because that would be
but a half-life, unliveable. That's what I
was. I embrace my darkness knowing that it
is smooth and calm and full. I feel the speckled
heat of my transient firedrops fall upon my face
It's been six years since I've seen my heart. What it
was once I will never know, but for now, I do.

My heart grows the shape of the fourteenth of November.

FIRE – or Finally seeing clearly for the first time in years, getting to really know my personality

I took a risky decision in October 2015 – to increase my medication. The reason why this was risky? My wedding was scheduled for Saturday 14th November 2015. I had improved since starting medication (ignoring a few major blips in March/April), but everything had plateaued and was even starting to gradually sink back down.

Bonfire night was a moment of revelation for me. It sounds like such a cliché, but increasing my medication caused me to feel like a huge weight had been lifted from me. Like I had been walking stooped for years and years, so long that I had almost forgotten. The lifting set me free.

I suddenly had the ability to actually see who I was as a person, the real me from out of the mist. I am naturally pensive, and sometimes too serious, but I am also incredibly daft, batty, singing silly words to tunes, playing with my kitty, dancing around my kitchen.

But the most important part of my identity that I could see with almost unnerving clarity was that I was loved.

There is no hand-written original for this piece, as I wrote this on my laptop, sat in my favourite armchair, with my pretty kitty on the windowsill and my now-husband reading on the sofa.

Never before had I felt so content, so happy, and so loved.

My biggest thanks, of course, go to Dan. My new husband, you are genuinely the best person I've ever known. I love you more than I ever thought possible, and you make every cliché I've ever heard about love seem fresh and new. I can't believe we're married, and I feel so lucky that I get to spend my life with you. Every day I write the story of my life in colours, and today is the purest white, with every beautiful colour rolled into one. Thank you for marrying me, darling.

I

love

you.

WHITE – or Yes, I know it's sappy to include my wedding speech, but it truly was the best day of my life so far

The opening of my wedding speech:

> Hello, everyone! For those of you who know me, it'll come as no surprise that I'm having a speech.

I'm a huge fan of tradition, but I've always been bossy and involved, ever since I was a child. However, the wedding speech wasn't about that – well, not entirely. I wanted everyone to know how amazing I thought they all were, and what an incredible day I was having, a day that was worth every bit of the build-up that we had given it.

And it was for Dan. He has been the constant presence in my life, keeping me sane and seeing me through everything, no matter how hard. To me, white is purity and perfection, and that also means him. Getting married is, and always will be, the best thing I've ever done.

I am weighted. Steel bones girded with concrete flesh. In my eye is the bathtub. My thumbs make way for ribbons as cracked shells become desirous steel. Carved lines in the left, such as I am right-handed. The lock holds but I succumb to the cries. Naked and shivering, powerless yet living - that is my wager. I lose my grip in an untimely skirmish; my mind roars, impotent. Cloths staunch and I am limp. Failure. Yet to see the wonder; I only see black. My mind is the void and I scream with the dark. I wear so many ribbons - neck, wrists, thigh. Highly strung from the stairs. One two three. Twice that bathtub. I am away, far away. But the screaming void has once more opened and all I see are the blackest moments. Electric blue and human red mean nothing now. I teeter. Once I would fall. Twice. Three times. Now I cling to myself, peering over the precipice of the black. It sings to me. Screaming. Or I to it. Or both. Neither.

(It's all in your head.)

BLACK – or Even happiness can be distorted by black thoughts and memories

Late one night I couldn't sleep, and it was the remembrance of unhappy times that were keeping me awake. One of those nights where you can't seem to see anything but every bad thing that you've ever done. The worst for me was hurting myself, and trying to end all things.

After writing this in my study by lamplight, on ominously grey paper, I went and stood in the garden. I don't know how long I was out there, maybe an hour, but I just stood looking at the silhouetted trees in the distance.

I had to include this piece because it would be a lie not to. I nearly didn't, because my fear was that this would be the focal point of the collection – it's not often that people are so frank, and I see why. It's really difficult.

But these memories are important because they give me perspective. I value everything.

Everyone has dark thoughts, horrid memories that intrude on contentment. The challenge is to embrace them as a part of yourself, in the hope that that way, you can let them go.

My glasses are tinted orange. Imagine a warm hand on your shoulder. A purring cat by your side. A roaring fire, a cup of cocoa, a good book. Cliché after cliché, but goodness. Happiness. The best things in life are free. It's the little things that count. If it's not broke, why fix it? I won't reinvent the wheel while my life turns so smoothly. I'm happy. Content. Each word whispers slowly out — no rush. Relax. Sit in quiet contentment. Wrapped in a blanket tied up with strings of Dvořák. A glass of mango lassi, with a side

THINGS THAT MAKE ME HAPPY

- my ginger hair
- our sunbleached sofa
- dresses made by mum
- our marmalade & white mog
- 'Wild Tulip' Morris wallpaper
- My Miffy lunchbox
- the arrival of the new hoover
- French Marigolds in bloom
- freshly squeezed orange juice
- butternut squash curry
- late summer dandelions

of charm. My lovely lucidity. My little house, bright, and warm, and happy. It's not a cliché to me. It's a welcome change. A seaside holiday after months of grey. Simply.

These are the things that make me happy.

ORANGE – or Happiness, contentment, and the warm fuzzy feelings only clichés can describe

It was of paramount importance to me that I wrote about the colour that expresses happiness to me. I'm not a gloomy character – I'm hopelessly optimistic, amused and entertained by the littlest things, and always trying to see the best in everyone.

This piece was actually the hardest to write. I started with a list of everything I loved related to my colour of happiness, orange. But every time after that that I attempted to put pen to paper, I stalled, with only clichés filling my mind.

Happiness has been written about hundreds of thousands of times, and the reason why clichés exist is because they're often true. Happiness isn't an original feeling, unique to me alone. Why should I strive to present it that way? So instead I have embraced the clichés. In this way, I feel that it is perhaps the most honest piece in this collection. Simplistic, unmediated and true.

I never thought that I would need a tour guide for inside my head. When I meditate I think of meadows, woodland. My sanctuary of thought is painted green. Where I can look inside, open the dated spreadsheets of my past and think - really think this time. Not to muse or dwell, not to sink into the melancholy mire of memory. Just to think. Sitting a little way away from the hard-drive of my brain lets the sun shine in. Sometimes we confuse 'most often', for 'favourites', but for me that's never true. If I did have a backspace button of the brain, would it work? Or would I make the same mistakes again? That's what memories try for: making fresh the once upon a time. Yet, each time we recall one, it changes. Gets better, gets worse, gets weird. Green helps. Like a filter over a magic picture that finally lets you see the spaceship, then you don't need the filter any more. That is my blessed clarity. Seeing it, you forget about the picture. I've solved the puzzle. I don't need the filter anymore. I can see the spaceship; I can fly away.

GREEN – or Guided introspection, mindfulness, and the goodness of therapy

Journaling is something that has always perplexed me. The idea is so simple, and with my love of writing, seemingly easy to carry out. But every journal I've ever had peters out half way through. I'm a planner, a diarist, but not a journal-keeper. Instead of day to day truths, ruminations and reflections, an old purple journal with numbered pages (1 to 120) hold my last two colourscapes – green and purple.

Pages 45 through 49 are written in green rollerball, thinking about thinking.

It's true what people say about therapy being a safe space – having another person there allows you to visit the worst points in your life without leaving yourself stuck in the memories. My therapist, Jill, sometimes says things that seem blatantly obvious in retrospect, but my ever-present response is always: of course! How did I never see that before?

Green is not being told who you are. It is the safe guidance to let you see it for yourself. It's not the answer to the puzzle, but sometimes a small clue is exactly what you need to get there.

I've always wanted to rule the world. Not in a maniacal 'wars and armies' way. But I want to do everything I can do and be everything I can be. Be the best that I can be. I'm a bossy little madam sometimes, and I don't have soft elbows. I am a whirling dervish of creation and there's nothing I can't do. With a checklist at my hand and a dustsheet at my feet, I've made magic from mayhem. I'm far from perfect, but damn it, I _try_. Maybe that gets me down. Sure. But I pick up the pieces that have shaved off my shoulders and decoupage them back on with super strength glue. I'm way off perfect, but I'm working on it. And in my purple power suit? I'm unstoppable.

PURPLE – or Feeling strong, confident, like I could rule the world or do ANYTHING

Page 51 through 54 of torn-out sheets from an old journal written in purple rollerball show me at the best that I can be.

Throughout my life, I have tried to do things – I've run school councils, played in every band, orchestra and choir available, written minutes, chaired meetings, organised various venues and studied two degrees at the same time. I LOVE doing things.

Writing, reading, making, doing, crafting, cleaning, dancing, singing, helping, honing, acting, advising, booking, climbing, swimming, weeding, playing, laughing, and, most of all, creating.

Purple is the colour that gives me strength – it makes me feel strong, independent; like I could take on the world and win. Everyone needs something to give them inspiration, and for me, that's purple.

After eight months, I'm now reducing my medication, and to stay strong I'm going to need every scrap of purple that I can find. That's why this colourscape closes this collection – right now, I'm ready to take on the world and to take on myself. I'm ready to roll.

Author's note:
The colourscapes listed below are text-only versions of the twelve
previous, for ease of reading.

GREY

I am grey. Some think that grey is unease, conflict, difficulty.
Perhaps it is. It is also nothing. White is too pure, unaltered to cradle
the dead-weight burden of nothing. Light grey, wisps like mists of
the moor. I am here, but only just. I am real, but only just. Mist
weighs heavier on your skin than raindrops. My heart trembles
while my pulse cannot match up. I am a parody of the Thinker,
frozen into grey. Solid now, anchored to the ground by the nothing
that has permeated my flesh, solidifying. The world around is green
and brown, flashes of golden yellow shot through with piercing cries
of young at play. I am rooted; yet, like any deadened bough, with life
comes buds. Piercing harder than any cry. I am shot through with
silver and my heart breathes. I am heavy, I am chains, I am cold. I
am the silver birch and the moon. No colour is ever what it seems in
the ever-changing light, and in the dusk I shine.

YELLOW-GREY

I don't believe in the beauty of a cloudless sky. My eyes, desperate
for colour, will prickle with static until I look away. I love when
you cannot see the sun, but the sunlight powders the tips of the
clouds with warmth. I am that pale yellow. Soft and warm. Musky
darkness still teases the horizon, but threaded through with ribbons
of gold. At peace. Voices echo through the silence and I feel a
gentle hum beside me. Here I can rest, beside myself. I can see the
storm clouds ahead, but the yellow softens them, makes them safe.
Hushes them to wait, slow. Not today, they say. I envelop my mind
in the brushed cotton clouds as we rattle along. I look to my own
ring of gold. I am safe.

MURKY

Murky. I can't see what the colours may be through the smog. The mundane viscosity, one plodding foot after another, heavily bursting each vacuumed step before sealing down once more with a shuck. It is a swamp, I can feel it. Half expected gas lamps shine in my distance, teasing me. Even if I did not know better than to follow them, I couldn't. I am a willow, rooted and weeping. The air is close; it breathes with me.

What dusk is dusk? I lose my senses in the dirge of murky colours. No time, no time. However, I never feel alone. I am surrounded, other rooted trees and swamp-stricken survivors. We are each to our own, but it is... comforting? The close air breathes me, rising and falling my chest. I close my eyes.

GLITTER

Glittering shimmering starbursts and opalescent scattered showers. Raindrops of colour mottle and evaporate together. Always perfect yet never enough and somehow too much. Somehow.

After, an oyster lies open, its thick pink tongue bedding a tiny pearl. Iridescent with echoes of its birth. Creation is wonderful, but, like all wonder, bridges itself with downy fear. The fear of the broken oyster. The clouded pearl. Not yet ripe.

A sigh.

Warm and awakened.

Waiting.

BROWN

Steadiness is hard to explain. It's not exactly a colour. It belongs to nature and is visible even on the coldest, gloomiest morning. The dominant colour is brown, but the magical thing about steadiness is that it is reflective. It helps you see yourself, understand that you are stronger than you let yourself believe and that you can weather the storm. I am the teal duck bobbing on a glassy moat. I am the pair of Canada Geese patrolling the water. I am each and every tree - oak, pine, chestnut, sycamore - decidedly deciduous, shaking my russet curls and watching the leaves fall. Caught in a blizzard of leaves, the wind whips and whirls them from the ground, forbidden to settle. Almost more alive, floating aloft the breeze, no longer chained by stem and twig. I wonder what colour I shall be when I twist myself free of my hanging stem. The leaves have so many faces that dance before my eyes - watery-eyed grandmothers, discontented adolescents, absent-minded stepfathers, cancer-ridden cousins. Not everyone grows old. Some leaves fall still green, whereas a withered mahogany-coloured maple may still cling to its bough. Once upon a time I would have wept for those leaves but now, I don't know. I can't unsee their beauty. I saw a family before, throwing piles of leaves at one another in lieu of snowballs. All metaphors are imperfect. But that moment was. I am the breadcrumbs thrown by a smiling child to a paddle of eager ducks. I am the leaves thrust into a not-quite unsuspecting face. I am each and every tree that births and sheds, year on year, ephemeral.

I live.

BLUE

Azure is a beautiful word, but the romantic in me favours powder blue. It feels delicate on the lips, not fruity and exotic. I am not a beach sky in the Mediterranean. I am an English meadow. My thoughts are scrunched into tight little origami dragonflies, ricocheting through me. I am a young soul drifting through an old life. After a summer storm the sky may clear to the inspiration of Turner – he could never stand me. Men and their mothers. I do not feel real. I am so living and yet so still. I feel like a shook bottle laid out in the sun. Will I fizz or am I flat? I am Schrodinger's soda.

FIRE

The shape of my heart is the fifth of November. I often write of the darkness, but I realise that I have long been wrong. It is not the darkness that is so bleak. It is the indecipherability. Like a fine grey mist clouding my way, darkness is only to fear when unconquerable. I feel like I finally understand. The tempest of my soul has finally begun to ease, to let me see the shapes underneath, and that shape is the fifth of November. Darkness and I are intrinsically linked, for one and for all. But I am not cloudy – no. I burn. I am life and I choose to revel in it. I watch the tips of lurid orange lick at the sky over hundreds of silhouetted heads, all so tall, my head thrown so far back in the hope of a glimpse of my heart. I am not the fire. Sometimes, I contain fire, but I am not strong enough to fuel the flames eternal. I am the embers thrown out by the flames that catch in the breeze and whisk upwards, alighting into the sky. The precious jewels encased by dusk, carelessly dancing without thought, nor mind, nor want. I am the navy-black sky, often pensive, knowingly anxious. I am laced with flecks of wondrous beauty, things I once thought were my only hope against the darkness. But I know. I know that I cannot be only the fiery echoes, because that would be but a half-life, unliveable. That's what I was. I embrace my darkness, knowing that it is smooth and calm and full. I feel the speckled heat of my transient firedrops fall upon my face.

It's been six years since I've seen my heart. What it was once, I will never know, but for now, I do.

My heart grows the shape of the fourteenth of November.

WHITE

My biggest thanks, of course, go to Dan. My new husband, you are genuinely the best person I've ever known. I love you more than I ever thought possible, and you make every cliché I've ever heard about love seem fresh and new. I can't believe we're married, and I feel so lucky that I get to spend my life with you. Every day I write the story of my life in colours, and today is the purest white, with every beautiful colour rolled into one. Thank you for marrying me, darling.

I love you.

BLACK

I am weighted. Steel bones girded with concrete flesh. In my eye is the bathtub. My thumbs make way for ribbons as cracked shells become desirous steel. Carved lines in the left, such as I am right-handed. The lock holds but I succumb to the cries. Naked and shivering, powerless yet living – that is my wager. I lose my grip in an untimely skirmish; my mind roars, impotent. Cloths staunch and I am limp. Failure. Yet to see the wonder; I only see black. My mind is the void and I scream with the dark. I wear so many ribbons – neck, wrists, thigh. Highly strung from the stairs. One two three. Twice that bathtub. I am away, far away. But the screaming void has once more opened and all I see are the blackest moments. Electric blue and human red mean nothing now. I teeter. Once I would fall. Twice. Three times. Now I cling to myself, peering over the precipice of the black. It sings to me. Screaming. Or I to it. Or both. Neither.

(It's all in your head.)

ORANGE

Things that make me happy:

- my ginger hair
- our sunbleached sofa
- dresses made by mum
- our marmalade and white mog
- 'Wild Tulip' Morris wallpaper
- my Miffy lunchbox
- the arrival of the new hoover
- French Marigolds in bloom
- freshly squeezed orange juice
- late summer dandelions
- butternut squash curry

My glasses are tinted orange. Imagine a warm hand on your shoulder. A purring cat by your side. A roaring fire, a cup of cocoa, a good book. Cliché after cliché, but goodness. Happiness. The best things in life are free. It's the little things that count. If it's not broke, why fix it? I won't reinvent the wheel while my life turns so smoothly. I'm happy. Content. Each word whispers slowly out – no rush. Relax. Sit in quiet contentment. Wrapped in a blanket tied up with strings of Dvorjak. A glass of mango lassi, with a side of charm. My lovely lucidity. My little house, bright, and warm, and happy. It's not a cliché to me. It's a welcome change. A seaside holiday after months of grey. Simply.

These are the things that make me happy.

GREEN

I never thought that I would need a tour guide for inside my head. When I meditate I think of meadows, woodland. My sanctuary of thought is painted green. Where I can look inside, open the dated spreadsheets of my past and think – really think this time. Not to muse or dwell, not to sink into the melancholy mire of memory. Just to think.

Sitting a little way away from the hard-drive of my brain lets the sun shine in. Sometimes we confuse 'most often' for 'favourites', but for me that's never true. If I did have a backspace button of the brain, would it work? Or would I make the same mistakes again? That's what memories try for: making fresh the once upon a time. Yet, each time we recall one, it changes. Gets better, gets worse, gets weird. Green helps. Like a filter over a magic picture that finally lets you see the spaceship, then you don't need the filter any more. That is my blessed clarity. Seeing it, you forget about the picture. I've solved the puzzle. I don't need the filter anymore. I can see the spaceship; I can fly away.

PURPLE

I've always wanted to rule the world. Not in a maniacal 'wars and armies' way. But I want to do everything I can do and be everything I can be. Be the best that I can be. I'm a bossy little madam sometimes, and I don't have soft elbows. I am a whirling dervish of creation and there's nothing I can't do. With a checklist at my hand and a dustsheet at my feet, I've made magic from mayhem. I'm far from perfect, but damn it, I try. Maybe that gets me down. Sure. But I pick up the pieces that have shaved off my shoulders and decoupage them back on with super strength glue. I'm way off perfect, but I'm working on it. And in my purple power suit? I'm unstoppable.

Acknowledgements

This book could not have been produced without the help, love and support of so many people.

From the Manchester Writing School, my thanks go to Adam Dalton and Nicholas Royle, two tutors who have given me such support and courage in my abilities – as Adam said, all I needed to do was to sit down and write a damn good book. My MA course-mates have provided invaluable help, and I hope my feedback to you has been as useful as your help to me. Dr Holly Jones of Ratbot Publishing, you've been so fantastic with your help and support, particularly with the technicalities of first-time publishing! I have been buoyed by the support of the clans Barker and Magnone, and I hope to have done you all proud.

Special thanks go to Louise Theodosiou, for without her initial idea and encouragement, this book may never have been written. And, of course, to my husband, Dan. Supporting me through the best of times and the worst of times, helping me wrestle with Inkscape, spotting typos, and making endless cups of tea. I couldn't have done this without you.

Finally, my eternal gratitude to YOU, reader, for picking up this book and taking a chance on an aspiring young author. Whether I know you or not, this endeavour would be fruitless without your support, and for that, you have my most heartfelt thanks.